STEP-BY-STEP

50 Recycled Crafts for Kids

STEP-BY-STEP

50 Recycled Crafts for Kids

Marion Elliot

Photographs by John Freeman

This edition published in 1996 by
SMITHMARK Publishers a division of U.S. Media Holdings Inc.
16 East 32nd Street, New York, NY 10016.

SMITHMARK books are available for bulk purchase for sales
promotion and for premium use. For details write or call
the Manager of Special Sales, SMITHMARK Publishers Inc.
16 East 32nd Street, New York, NY, 10016; (212) 5326600

Produced by Anness Publishing Limited
1 Boundary Row
London SE1 8HP

Printed and bound in Hong Kong

CONTENTS

INTRODUCTION

Just think of all the different things we all throw away without a second thought! It is estimated that we produce several times our own weight in rubbish every year. We haven't even used some of the things that we dispose of, because they are used to package our everyday items, such as food, drinks, soap powder, toothpaste and washing-up detergent.

Instead of wasting all these lovely pieces of plastic, paper and cardboard, it is much better to make them into something new, such as the fun toys, games, jewellery and decorations that are in this book. All the projects are made using things that you might throw away every day and the best news is that most of the materials are free. You will be able to make a lot of the projects by yourself, but you will need adult help for some of them, so be sure to ask when the project says to do so. Don't worry if you can't find exactly the same materials to recycle as appear in each project; the best bit about using packaging is that there is so much to choose from that you can pick the shapes and colours that you like the best!

Recycling

This book shows you lots and lots of exciting ways to use waste materials to make fun projects. Once you have started to collect junk, you will realize just how much packaging, newspaper, cardboard and plastic we all throw away every day.

It takes a lot of the earth's precious raw materials, such as metal, wood and oil, to make paper, bottles, drinks cans and plastics. Huge amounts of fuel and energy are used to turn the raw materials into these products. It is very wasteful to throw so much away, especially as a lot of our rubbish is packaging, and is only used once, but you can actually help to look after the earth and its resources by recycling the things that nobody wants.

If we take the trouble to put old bottles, newspapers and tins in special banks, they can be made into new ones. This helps to use the earth's resources more wisely and it makes you feel good too!

Apart from recycling your household waste in special banks, you can also re-use it to make lots of exciting things. Before you throw something away, look at it carefully and ask yourself a few questions. Is it an interesting shape or a nice colour? Does it suggest an idea for a project to you? Can you think of an ingenious way of making it into something new and completely different? If the answer to any of these is yes, hang on to it and start a collection of interesting materials. Here are some of the things to look out for.

Cardboard tubes and rolls
These can be found in the middle of rolls of silver foil, toilet paper and sticky tape. They are also used to protect rolled paper. Tubes are great for making models, such as telescopes and for creating junk sculptures.

Coloured cord, thread and string
This is good for stringing beads, making mobiles, joining sections of models and puppets, and hanging decorations. Collect discarded scraps from parcels and packages.

Corrugated cardboard
This is great for making models, frames and jewellery. Corrugated cardboard comes in different thicknesses and can be one or more layers deep. Keep your eyes open for discarded TV and computer boxes when you are out because they are a great source of good-quality cardboard.

Elastic bands
Elastic bands come in lots of different colours and sizes. Some are very thin and springy, which are the kind you need for projects like the pinball machine. Others are thicker and stronger, and are helpful for holding a project together while the glue dries.

Fabric scraps
Fabric can be quite expensive to buy and you will usually only need a little bit for each project. If you know anyone who sews, ask them to keep scraps for you.

Newspapers
We throw away tons and tons of newspaper every day. It comes in all sorts of different colours, thicknesses and sizes. It is very good for making papier-mâché, folding into hats and covering your work surface.

Plastic bags
Some bags are brightly coloured and are good for making puppets' clothes. They are also good for keeping your collection of materials tidy! Plastic bags can be very dangerous, never leave them where babies and young children might find them.

Plastic bottles
These come in lots of different shapes and sizes and can be brightly coloured or clear. They are good for making musical instruments and toys like puppets and skittles.

Paper clips
Paper clips come in lots of different sizes and colours. They are good for decorating junk sculptures, especially robots, and are useful for holding projects together while the glue dries.

Plastic food containers
These come in many interesting shapes and some are very decorative. They make great moulds for papier-mâché and are also good for adding details to large models.

Scrap paper
It takes a lot of trees to make paper, so don't waste scraps! Coloured paper is good for making all sorts of party decorations, papier-mâché and greetings cards.

From left to right, top row: *cardboard tubes and rolls, coloured cord, thread and string, corrugated cardboard, elastic bands*
middle row: *paper clips, fabric scraps, scrap paper, plastic food containers*
bottom row: *newspapers, plastic carrier bags, plastic bottles.*

Materials and Equipment

These are just some of the materials used in this book. Some you will already have, others you may have to buy.

coloured sticky-paper dots

coloured foil

sweet wrappers

corks

Cardboard tubes
These come in a variety of sizes in the centres of toilet rolls, kitchen-paper rolls and rolls of silver foil.

Coloured cord, thin
This is very strong and is good for necklaces and hanging mobiles.

Coloured sticky-paper dots
These come in a variety of colours and sizes and are available from most stationers.

Corks
Corks are good for making small dolls, animals and other toys.

Cotton thread
This comes in lots of bright colours and thicknesses and is good for patchwork and sewing.

Darning needles
These are wide needles with large eyes and rounded ends that are not very sharp. Use them for sewing, for stringing beads and for threading elastic.

Elastic bands
These come in lots of colours and different lengths.

Elastic
It is possible to buy thin elastic in different colours, such as silver, gold and glitter-effect.

Fabric and felt scraps
Scraps of fabric and felt are useful for making fabric pictures, toys' clothes and patchwork. Felt comes in lots of lovely colours and doesn't fray.

Felt-tipped pens
These must be non-toxic. Felt-tipped pens are good for adding decoration to paper and card.

Masking tape
Masking tape is made from paper and is easy to remove after it has been stuck down.

Measuring tape
You sometimes need this for measuring fabric.

Natural objects
These include twigs, acorns and fir cones, which can be picked up in parks and during country walks. Always show an adult what you have found before you use it, to make sure that it is safe.

Paintbrushes
Paintbrushes come in a variety of sizes. Use a medium-thick brush for general painting and for applying glue. Use fine brushes to paint·more detailed designs.

Paints
These must be non-toxic. Poster paints are good because they come in lots of lovely colours.

Palette
A palette is a useful container for paint. If you don't have one, an old saucer or plastic carton is just as good.

Paper clips
Paper clips may be plain or patterned and come in lots of sizes. They are meant for holding pieces of paper together, but some may be colourful and

attractive enough to be used as decoration as well.

Paper glue
This must be non-toxic and comes in liquid or a solid stick.

Pencils
A soft pencil is useful for making tracings and transferring them to card and paper.

PVA (white) glue
This must be non-toxic. PVA (white) glue is very sticky and is good for gluing cardboard and fabric. It can also be mixed with poster paints to make them stick to plastic surfaces. It is useful as a varnish and, if you dilute it, you can use it to make papier-mâché.

Ruler
A ruler is useful for measuring and drawing straight lines.

Scissors
These should be of the type that are made specially for children and have rounded blades.

Silver and coloured foil
Silver foil comes on long rolls and is good for making jewellery. Coloured foil covers sweets (candy) and biscuits (cookies).

Sticky tape
This can be used for sticking paper, card and foil.

Strong glue
This must be non-toxic and solvent-free. Strong glue is useful for sticking heavy cardboard and holding awkward joints together.

PVA (white) glue

silver
foil

paper
glue

palette

paintbrushes

fabric
scraps

paints

strong glue

felt-tipped
pens

pencils

wooden
spoons

ruler

scissors

natural
objects

cardboard tubes

coloured cord and threads

sticky tape

elastic bands

darning needles

pins

paper
clips

masking tape

TECHNIQUES

Tracing

Some of the projects in this book have patterns that you can transfer directly to paper or use to make templates. Tracing is the quickest way to make copies of a pattern so that you can easily transfer it to another piece of paper or cardboard.

 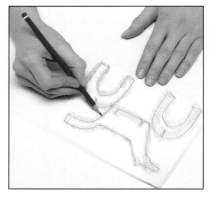

1 Lay your piece of tracing paper on the pattern and use a soft pencil to draw over the image, making a dark line. Turn the sheet of tracing paper over and place it on a scrap of paper. Scribble over the lines with your pencil.

2 Turn the tracing right-side up again and place it on an appropriate piece of paper or card. Carefully draw over the lines to transfer the tracing to the paper or cardboard.

3 Lift up the tracing paper and you will see that your outline is now on the paper or cardboard.

Scaling-up

Sometimes you will want to make a project bigger than the template given. It's easy to make it larger. This is known as scaling-up. Use a scale of, say, one square on the template to two squares on the graph paper. You may use a different scale depending on the size you want.

1 If you wish to copy a template that is not printed on a grid, trace it and transfer it to graph paper. If the template you have chosen does appear on a grid, proceed directly to step 2.

2 Using an appropriate scale, enlarge the template onto a second piece of paper, copying the shape from each smaller square to the larger square.

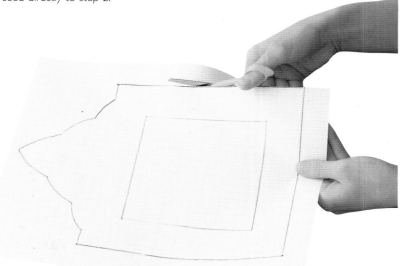

3 Cut out the template and transfer it to card (posterboard) or paper.

Papier-mâché

Papier-mâché is made by shredding paper, usually old newspapers, and combining it with glue. The paper can be used in a number of ways to make a huge variety of objects which are either useful or just for decoration.

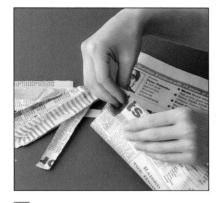

1 For most projects, paper should be torn into fairly short strips approximately 2 cm (¾ in) wide.

2 Mix some non-toxic PVA (white) glue with water to the consistency of single (light) cream.

3 Papier-mâché can be pressed into lightly greased moulds or wrapped around cardboard shapes like this.

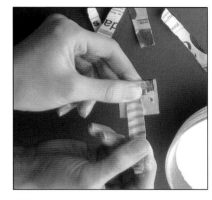

4 To cover smaller shapes, use small, thin pieces of newspaper.

5 Your papier-mâché object may have a slightly rough surface when it has dried out. To make it uniformly smooth, lightly rub the paper with fine sandpaper.

6 Prime your papier-mâché with two coats of non-toxic white paint to conceal the newsprint surface before decorating.

Printing with Foam Rubber Stamps

Simple stamps can be cut from sheets of thin foam rubber and stuck onto cardboard bases. Use these recycled stamps to make your own special greetings cards, or even to decorate your walls.

1 To make the stamps, cut several rectangles of heavy cardboard measuring 5 × 6 cm (2 × 2¼ in). Cut an equal number of smaller rectangles measuring 1.5 × 6 cm (⅝ × 2¼ in) to form the handles. Stick the handles to the tops of the bases with strong glue.

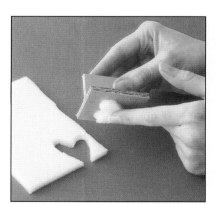

2 Draw the stamp motif onto foam rubber. Cut it out with scissors and glue it to the cardboard base. Allow to dry thoroughly.

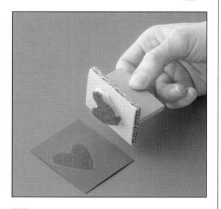

3 Mix paint with water to a stiff consistency. Gently dip the stamp in the paint and then press it onto medium-weight paper or thin card (posterboard).

Painting on Plastic

All the projects in this book involve recycling and some are made from plastic bottles and yogurt cartons. Sometimes you may want to paint these but ordinary poster paint will not stick to plastic. However, if you add glue to the paint it will be sticky and will cover the plastic well.

1 Put some ordinary poster paint into a palette or small dish.

2 Pour in a little PVA (white) glue. Carefully mix the paint and the glue, until they are thoroughly mixed together.

3 Wash your plastic bottle in warm soapy water and dry thoroughly. Apply the paint mixture over the surface of the bottle, taking care to spread the paint smoothly. Wash your brush thoroughly, as soon as you have finished.

Flattening and Cutting up a Box

Cardboard can be used for papier-mâché frames among other things. Old boxes are the best source, and you can flatten them out easily.

1 Remove any tape that is holding the box together and press it flat.

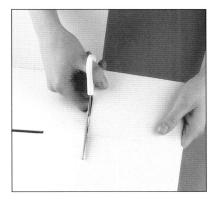

2 Cut the box into pieces, ready for use in your various projects.

Re-using Foil Wrappers

Coloured foil is great for decorations, and you don't have to buy it specially. Save old sweet (candy) wrappers and cases made of pretty colours, and cut them into different shapes.

1 Flatten the wrappers and cases and smooth them out. Cut them up for use in your projects.

Removing a Label from a Bottle

Plastic bottles can be used for all kinds of projects. You will want to wash them thoroughly.

1 Fill a washing-up bowl with warm soapy water.

2 Soak the bottle in the water for approximately ten minutes.

3 Peel the label off the bottle. If the label is still sticking to the bottle, soak it in the water for a little longer.

QUICK AND EASY RECYCLING IDEAS

COAT-HANGER TRIANGLE

If you want to make a triangle quickly, all you need is a metal coat-hanger, a teaspoon and a length of ribbon. The coat-hanger will make a clear sound when you strike it and you could make several triangles for your friends and form a small band!

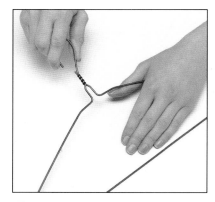

1 Ask an adult to bend over the hook of a metal coat-hanger for you, to make a closed loop at the top.

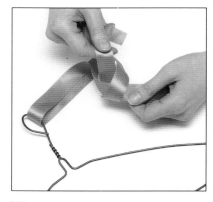

2 Cut a length of ribbon or cord and tie it around the loop. Tie the ends of the ribbon together to make a hanger, so that you can hold your triangle.

3 Hold your triangle in one hand and strike it with a metal teaspoon, to make a chiming sound.

WOODEN SPOON PUPPET

This is a really quick and easy way to make a wooden spoon puppet. All you need is a wooden spoon, a plastic carrier bag and some felt-tipped pens. However, don't give the puppet to very young children, because plastic bags can be dangerous.

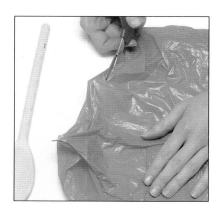

1 Lay a brightly coloured plastic carrier bag flat. Snip off one bottom corner of the bag to make a small hole.

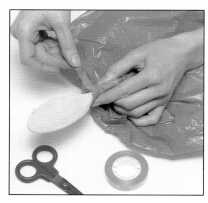

2 Push the handle of a wooden spoon through the hole into the bag, as far as it will go. Tape the edges of the bag around the top of the spoon to keep the bag in place.

3 Using felt-tipped pens, draw your puppet's face on the front of the spoon. You can also draw buttons or patterns on the front of the bag to make the puppet's body more interesting.

LITTLE SHAKER

It is easy to make a little percussion instrument that is small enough to fit in your hand. This one is made from two brightly coloured yogurt pots, filled with dried rice. It makes quite a lot of noise when you shake it!

1 Wash and dry the yogurt pots thoroughly. Pour a small handful of rice into one of them.

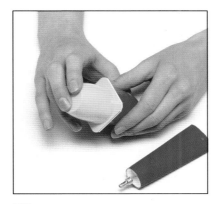

2 Spread a little glue around the tops of the yogurt pots. Place the second yogurt pot on top of the first and press the two pots firmly together. Let the glue dry thoroughly before you play your shaker.

MAKING SILVER FOIL BEADS

Silver foil makes great beads. You can squash small pieces, roll them into balls and then glue them to things like pendants to make decorations. Or you can cut thin strips of foil and roll them up, to make long, thin beads that are good for stringing into necklaces.

1 Squash and roll scraps of silver foil, to make small round beads. Press one side of each bead to make a flat surface, so that you can glue them to things as decoration.

2 To make long, thin beads, cut a piece of silver foil into strips about 2.5 cm (1 in) wide. Lay a pencil at one end of a foil strip and carefully roll the strip around the pencil, to make a tube. Tape the ends of the bead together, to stop it from unravelling.

QUICK PAPER BAG MASK

If you want a mask quickly and don't have much time, you can make a really good one from a large brown paper bag. You must never be tempted to make one from a plastic carrier bag, though, as they are very dangerous. Before you start the mask, make sure the bag is not too small for your head, or so big that you get lost in it.

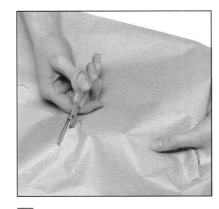

1 Draw three holes on the front of the mask and cut them out to make openings for your eyes and mouth.

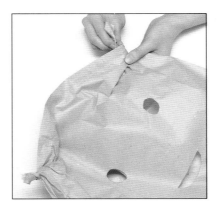

2 Roll up the bottom of the paper bag two or three times, so that it comes down just past your chin. Twist the top corners to make ears.

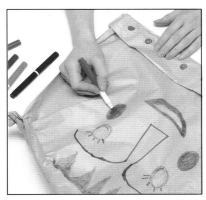

3 Decorate both the front and back of your mask, using felt-tipped pens, in an exciting and colourful way.

TEMPLATES

Fabric Scrap Picture
(⅔ actual size)

Sponge-flower Hair Band
(actual size)

Storage Chest
(actual size)

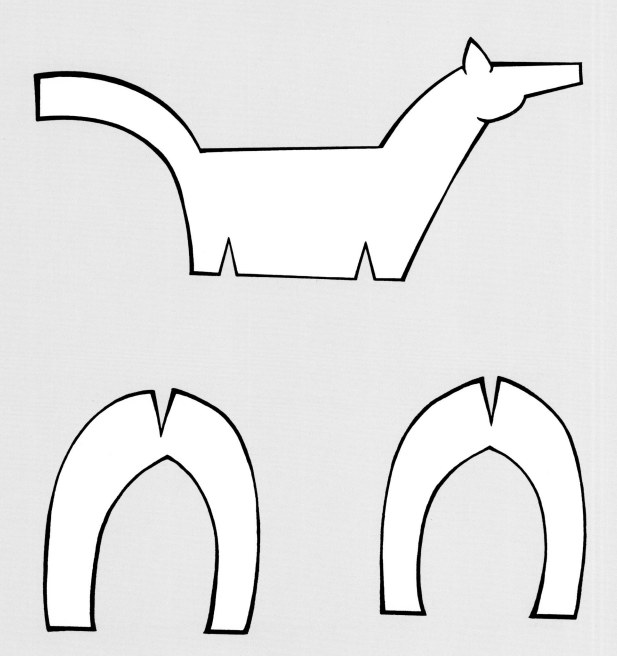

Peg Cowboy
(actual size)

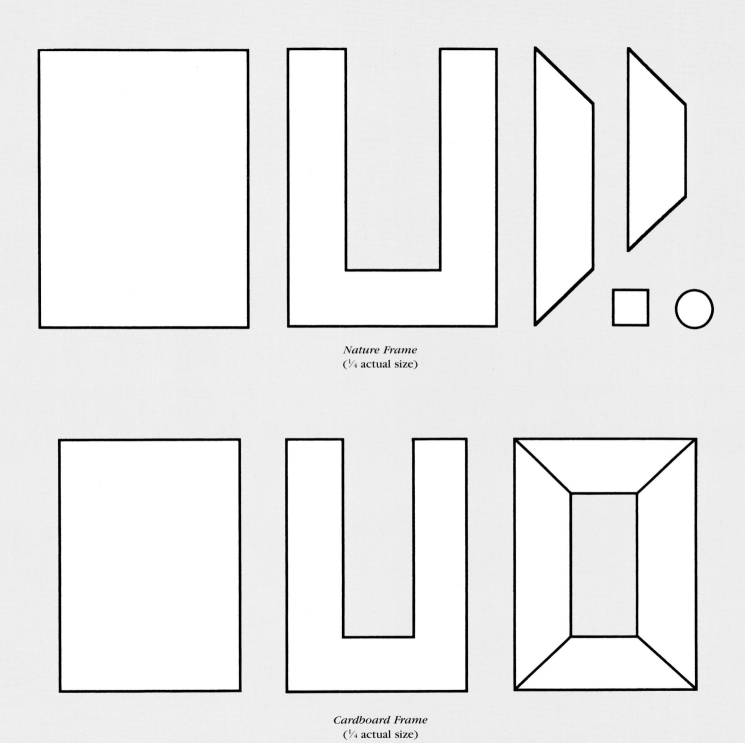

Nature Frame
(¼ actual size)

Cardboard Frame
(¼ actual size)

Toys and Puppets

Junk Robot

All you need to make this fabulous robot is a washing-powder box, a plastic cup, some washing line, washing-up sponges and toilet-roll tubes. Its features and control panel are added with various bits and pieces, such as bottle tops, yogurt pots and a safety pin, so keep an eye on the kitchen bin for useful robot parts!

RECYCLING TIP
Silver foil can be used more than once. If it has been used for food carefully wash it with soapy water and a sponge and then leave it to dry.

YOU WILL NEED
strong, non-toxic glue
4 toilet-roll tubes
washing line
elastic bands
plastic cup
silver foil
scissors
sticky tape
washing-powder box
washing-up sponges
2 small yogurt pots
2 thick sponge scourers
3 round plastic scourers
bottle caps and other
  bits and pieces
2 metal washers
safety pin
foil pie dishes (pans)

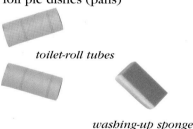

toilet-roll tubes

washing-up sponge

foil dishes

plastic scourer

sticky tape

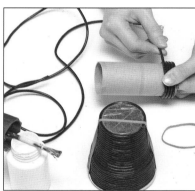

1 Put a little glue on the tops and bottoms of the toilet-roll tubes. Wrap washing line around the tubes. Hold it in place with elastic bands while the glue dries. Do the same to the plastic cup.

2 Cut a piece of silver foil that is large enough to cover the washing-powder box. Loosely crumple the foil, to give it a crinkly surface, and tape it around the box.

3 Cut two circles from washing-up sponge and glue them to one end of two of the toilet-roll tubes. Glue a small yogurt pot to the other end of both tubes to make the robot's arms.

4 To make the robot's legs, glue a thicker scourer to one end of the two remaining toilet-roll tubes. Stretch a round plastic scourer over each end of the tubes.

5 Glue plastic bottle caps and other bits and pieces to the front of the box to make the controls. Glue two metal washers and a safety pin to the front of the plastic cup to make the robot's face.

6 Glue the cup to the top of the box and put a plastic scourer over it to make the neck. Glue the legs to the bottom and one arm to each side; hold in place with elastic bands until the glue dries.

Wild West Ranch

Every cowboy needs a ranch and here's one to be proud of. The ranch house is a cardboard box covered with pieces of corrugated cardboard, which go well with the lolly-stick roof and make the house look as if it's made from wood. The floor is made from coarse sandpaper.

RECYCLING TIP
It might take you a long time to eat enough lollies for all these sticks so ask your friends to save theirs too.

YOU WILL NEED
ruler
scissors
corrugated cardboard
strong, non-toxic glue
cardboard box
brown and green poster paints
paintbrush
paint-mixing container
thin cardboard
sticky tape
lolly sticks
coloured paper
coarse sandpaper sheet

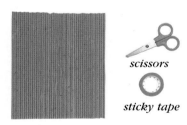

scissors

sticky tape

corrugated cardboard

paintbrush

lolly sticks

glue

poster paints

pencil   ruler

1 Cut four pieces of corrugated cardboard and glue them around the box. Paint the cardboard brown.

2 To make the roof, cut two pieces of thin card (posterboard) just longer than the box. Tape them together on the back, so they fold in a roof shape. Glue lolly sticks to both sides of the roof.

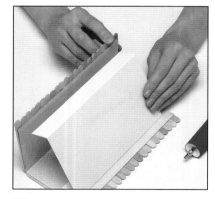

3 Cut a rectangle of thin card (posterboard) as long as the top of the box and 5 cm (2 in) wider. Fold over 2.5 cm (1 in) on either side to make flaps. Glue the card inside the roof to make a base. Glue the roof to the house.

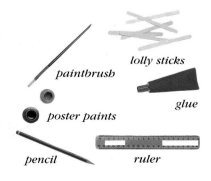

4 For windows, cut two squares of yellow paper; fold in four and cut a square out of the corner. Open it out and glue to the house. Cut a rectangle of corrugated cardboard for a door.

5 Cut a rectangle of corrugated cardboard the same size as the sandpaper. Glue the sheet of sandpaper to the cardboard.

6 To make the fence, cut a strip of corrugated cardboard 2.5 cm (1 in) high and long enough to glue around the base and paint green.

Peg (Clothespin) Cowboys

These cowboys are ready to ride the range on their dappled horses. They are made from old-fashioned wooden pegs and look very smart in their gingham shirts and spotted neckerchiefs. The horses are made from thin card (posterboard) and they can stand upright.

YOU WILL NEED
white, dark blue and red
  poster paints
paintbrushes
paint-mixing container
wooden clothes pegs
  (clothespins)
scissors
yellow, red and white
  paper scraps
strong, non-toxic glue
tracing paper
pencil
thin white card (posterboard)
felt-tipped pens

wooden clothes pegs

scissors

poster paints

pencil

felt-tipped pen

paintbrushes

paper scraps

glue

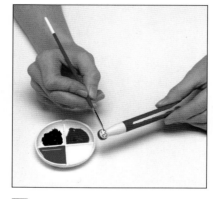

1 Paint the top of a peg (clothespin) white. Paint the bottom half dark blue to make the cowboy's jeans.

2 When the first coat of paint has dried, add details, such as the cowboy's face and the checks on his shirt, using poster paints.

3 Cut a hat from yellow paper. Fold up the edges and then glue the hat to the front of the cowboy's head. Cut a neckerchief from red paper and add spots with white paint. Glue the neckerchief around the cowboy's neck.

4 Cut two strips of white paper to make the cowboy's arms. Paint a hand at the end of each strip and add checks. Glue the arms to the cowboy's sides.

5 Trace the horse patterns from the front of the book. Lay the tracings face-down on thin white card (posterboard) and draw over the lines to transfer to the card. Cut out all the pieces.

6 Using felt-tipped pens, draw in the horse's face and its markings. Push the body into the slots in its legs. Sit the cowboy on his horse.

Space Station

If you like the idea of space travel, why not make yourself a floating space station like this one? It has a radar dish and a landing stage for you to park rockets and other spacecraft on. Look around for any interestingly-shaped odds and ends that would look good on your space station; paint them silver, and start building!

RECYLING TIP
You can use all sorts of different sized boxes but make sure the cardboard isn't too thick, if the boxes are too heavy the glue might not hold them together.

YOU WILL NEED
small and large cardboard boxes
paintbrush
paint-mixing container
silver poster paint
PVA (white) glue
4 paper bowls
cardboard tubes
2 round foil pie dishes (pans)
strong, non-toxic glue
2 yogurt pots
drinking straw
round cardboard carton
rectangular foil dish

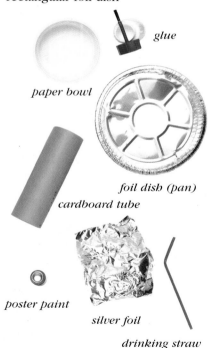

glue

paper bowl

foil dish (pan)

cardboard tube

poster paint

silver foil

drinking straw

I Paint the large cardboard box and the smaller one silver. You may have to paint the boxes twice to cover the cardboard properly.

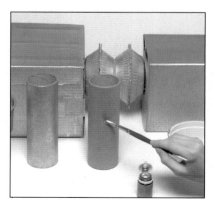

2 Glue the rims of two paper bowls together with PVA glue. Glue two more in the same way. Stick all four together. Paint them silver and glue them between the two boxes to make an airlock.

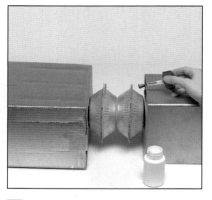

3 Paint one of the tubes silver. Glue the rims of the foil pie dishes (pans) together with strong glue; glue them to the top of the tube. Glue the tube to the larger box to make a landing stage.

4 Add a little PVA glue to the silver paint and paint the yogurt pots, one small and two large cardboard tubes silver. Glue one pot to the small tube. Stick this next to the landing pad.

5 Stick the tubes one each side of the larger box and the yogurt pot to the end. Cover the straw with silver foil and paint the round carton silver. Join them together and stick to the smaller box.

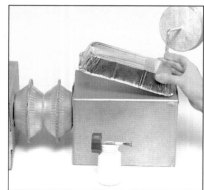

6 Stick the rectangular foil dish upside-down next to the aerial.

Tanker Truck

Collect different sizes of cardboard boxes and see which look most like a truck when they are put together.

YOU WILL NEED
4 long, thin cotton reels (spools)
4 small jam-jar lids
strong, non-toxic glue
drinking straws
scissors
thin cardboard scraps
square and rectangular cardboard boxes
2 short cotton reels (spools)
squeezy bottle
white paper
yellow, blue and red poster paints
paintbrushes
paint-mixing container

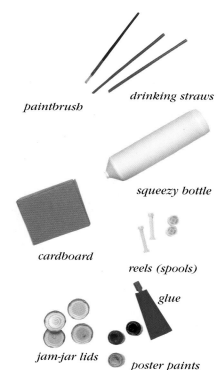

paintbrush

drinking straws

squeezy bottle

cardboard

reels (spools)

glue

jam-jar lids

poster paints

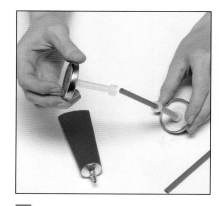

1 Glue a cotton reel (spool) to the centre of the inside of each jam-jar lid, or the wheels. Cut two lengths of straw about 4 cm (1½ in) longer than the widths of the cabin and trailer boxes to make axles. Glue each axle inside one of the cotton reels (spools) at each end.

2 Cut four strips of card measuring 5 cm (2 in) x 1.5 cm (½ in). Bend each strip into a U shape. Spread glue on one end and attach two to the bottom of the cabin and two to the bottom of the trailer. Place a pair of wheels inside each U shape. Glue the open side of the other end in place.

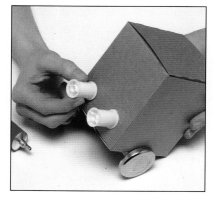

3 Glue the two short cotton reels (spools) to the back of the cabin. Spread glue on the other end and stick the trailer to them.

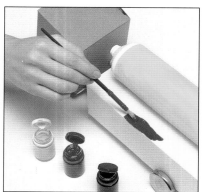

4 Glue a piece of white paper around the squeezy bottle. Glue the bottle to the top of the trailer to make a tanker. Decorate using poster paints.

Tin-can Stilts

Make a pair of these tin-can stilts and you'll be walking tall! Use very strong cans that can support your weight and choose those with removable lids, because they don't have a sharp rim. Ask an adult to file the edges of the holes smooth after they are punched, so they don't cut through the cord handles.

YOU WILL NEED
ruler
pencil
gift wrap
scissors
paper glue
2 strong tin cans, with
    removable lids
thick coloured cord
sticky tape

scissors

gift wrap

cord

tin can

sticky tape

glue

pencil

ruler

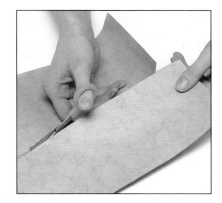

1 Measure and draw out two strips of gift wrap, the same width as the cans and long enough to fit around them. Cut out the strips.

2 Glue one paper strip around each can. Ask an adult to punch a hole in each side of the unopened end of each can, near the rim. Ask them to file the edges of the holes completely smooth.

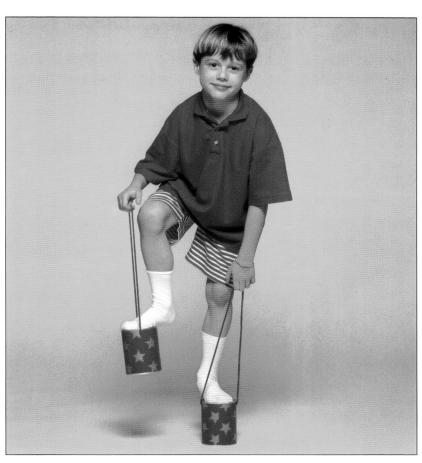

3 Cut two lengths of cord that are two-and-a-half times as long as the distance from your ankle to your knee. To make the handles, push the ends of the cords through the holes from the outside to the inside of the cans.

4 Tie a knot in the end of each handle to stop them pulling out of the holes. If the handles are the right length, tie an extra knot in the other end to keep them in place. If not, adjust the cord until they feel right.

Indoor Snowstorm

If you've saved some Christmas cake decorations and don't know what to do with them in the new year, why not use them to make a snowstorm? Glue them inside a clear plastic jar, add some water and a handful of glitter and you'll have a winter scene to remind you of Christmas. Make sure the jar lid fits tightly, so there's no chance of any of the water leaking out.

YOU WILL NEED
clear plastic jar, with lid
pencil
silver foil
scissors
strong, non-toxic glue
Christmas cake decorations, e.g.
  Santa Claus, reindeer and
  Christmas tree
water
gold glitter

water

scissors

silver foil

gold glitter

glue

Christmas decorations

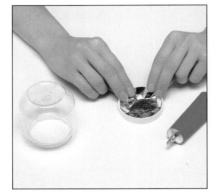

1 Wash and thoroughly dry the jar. Draw around the neck of the jar on a piece of silver foil. Cut out the circle of foil and glue it to the inside of the lid.

2 Glue Santa Claus, the reindeer and the Christmas tree to the lid and leave the glue to dry thoroughly overnight.

3 Fill the jar almost to the top with water. Carefully pour one heaped teaspoon of gold glitter into the water and stir it in.

4 Spread glue around the neck of the jar. Lower the decorations into the jar and screw the lid in place. When the lid is secure, turn the jar upside-down and shake it to see the snowstorm.

Paper-plate Cat Mask

Paper plates are great for making masks. You can either use them flat and cut holes for your eyes and mouth, or be a bit more ingenious and cut them to sit on your head.

YOU WILL NEED
pencil
paper plate
scissors
orange, blue, red and yellow
   poster paints
paintbrushes
paint-mixing container

paper plate

paintbrushes

poster paints

scissors

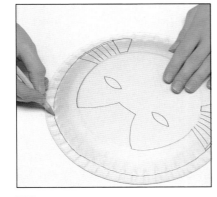

1 Using the pencil, draw the mask design on the back of the paper plate.

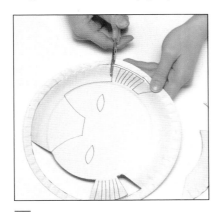

2 Cut out the mask. Ask an adult to cut out the eye holes for you.

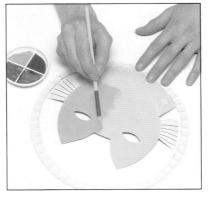

3 Paint the cat's face orange. Paint its collar blue, leaving four white dots to colour in later.

4 When the first coat of paint has dried, paint the cat's features on top and finish the collar.

Paper-bag Animal Mask

Plain paper bags are great for making masks quickly and easily. You can cut them into all sorts of different shapes and use felt-tipped pens to add exciting decoration. Collect brown-paper carrier bags to make masks too – they're stronger than paper bags and will last longer.

YOU WILL NEED
pencil
2 large paper bags
scissors
paper glue
orange, red and black
  felt-tipped pens

felt-tipped pens

paper bag

pencil

scissors

glue

1 Draw three holes on the front of your paper bag, for your eyes and mouth. Cut out the holes.

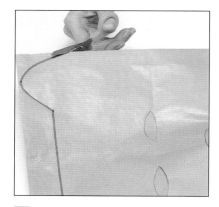

2 Draw two ears along the top edge of the bag and cut them out. Glue the top edges of the bag together again.

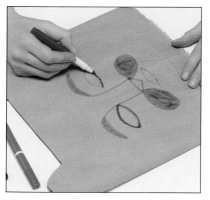

3 Draw the animal's face on the front of the bag, using felt-tipped pens. Draw red lines around the eyes so that they stand out strongly.

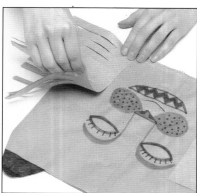

4 Cut three wide strips from another paper bag. Make long cuts along one long edge of each strip. Glue the uncut edges of the strips to the sides and top of the animal's head to make a mane.

Cotton Reel (Spool) Robot

This robot is made from cotton reels (spools) and foil pie dishes (pans). Cotton reels (spools) are great because the hole in the middle means they can easily be threaded together.

YOU WILL NEED
scissors
silver foil
17 small cotton reels (spools)
1 large cotton reel (spool)
sticky tape
darning needle
thin elastic
4 small foil pie dishes (pans)
paper clips
press studs
strong, non-toxic glue

glue

paper clips

press studs

silver foil

scissors

foil dishes (pans)

cotton reels (spools)

1 Cut strips of silver foil about 1.5 cm (½ in) wider than the reels (spools) and long enough to fit around them. Cover the reels (spools) with foil.

2 To make the lower body, thread a darning needle with elastic and tie a big knot in the end. Ask an adult to make a hole in the centre of two dishes (pans) and two holes in a third. Thread a dish onto the elastic; then three small reels (spools); then the dish with two holes; then three reels (spools); then a dish. Tie a knot in the end and cut the elastic.

3 Ask an adult to make a hole in the centre of the last dish. To make the upper body, tie a knot in the end of a piece of elastic; thread on three small reels (spools) and a large reel (spool) for the head. Secure with a paper clip.

4 To make an arm, tie a paper clip to the end of some elastic, thread on four small reels and tie a knot in the end. Glue the dishes together and attach the arms below the head. Use paper clips and press studs for its face and controls.

Space Cat

Greetings, earthlings! Collect small yogurt cartons to make this fun, spotted space cat. Its legs are coloured drinking straws and it stands on flat button feet. Try to find a suitable bottle cap like this one for its head, which has small points at the top that look just like ears.

RECYCLING TIP
Make sure you wash the yogurt cartons thoroughly in warm soapy water before you use them.

YOU WILL NEED
drinking straws
ruler
scissors
thin elastic
buttons
wooden beads
2 small yogurt cartons
strong, non-toxic glue
coloured sticky-paper dots
bottle cap
black felt-tipped pen

sticky-paper dots

glue   felt-tipped pen

thin elastic

yogurt pots

drinking straw

buttons

bottle cap

wooden beads

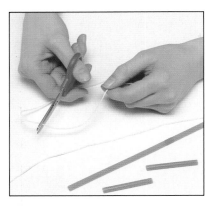

1 Cut four pieces of straw measuring 6 cm (2 in) long. Cut four pieces of thin elastic measuring 30 cm (12 in) long.

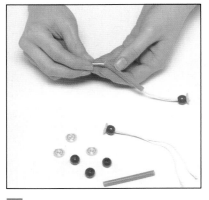

2 To make a leg, thread a piece of elastic through both holes in a button. Push the button to the centre of the elastic. Hold the ends together and thread on a wooden bead and a piece of straw. Repeat for the other legs.

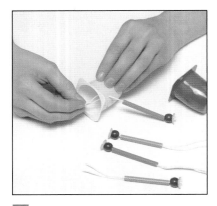

3 Ask an adult to make a hole in both sides of the yogurt cartons and in the end of one of them. Attach the legs to the cartons by pushing the ends of the elastic through the holes in the sides of the cartons and tying them tightly.

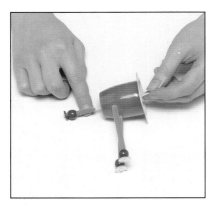

4 To make the tail, thread a button, a bead and a 2-cm (1-in) piece of straw onto a 20-cm (8-in) length of elastic. Push the ends through the hole in the end of the carton and knot tightly.

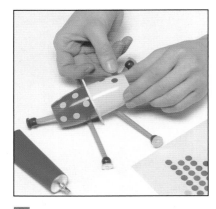

5 Spread glue along the top edges of both the cartons and stick them together. Add coloured sticky-paper dots to the cat's body for decoration.

6 Stick coloured dots to the top of the bottle cap to make the eyes and nose, draw pupils with the felt-tipped pen, and glue to the front of the body.

Television Set

Instead of watching the TV, why not make one
from a cardboard box and appear on it yourself?
Cover the box in silver foil, add an aerial and
present your first programme.

YOU WILL NEED
scissors
large cardboard box
pencil
ruler
silver foil
sticky tape
coloured paper
PVA (white) glue
foil pudding dish (pan)
2 knitting needles with
   rounded ends
3 bottle tops

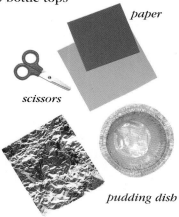

paper

scissors

pudding dish

silver foil

ruler

pencil

bottle tops

sticky tape

glue

knitting needles

1 Carefully cut the flaps from the top
of the cardboard box. Ask an adult to
help you if the cardboard is very thick.

2 Using a ruler, draw a large square
on one side of the box and ask an adult
to help you to cut it out. Leave enough
room for the control panel.

3 Cut lengths of silver foil. Loosely
crumple the foil to make a crinkled
surface and then tape the foil around
the box until the outside is covered.

4 Cut a piece of coloured paper
large enough to cover the inside of the
box opposite the opening. Glue it to the
inside of the box to make a coloured
background.

5 Spread glue around the edge of
the foil pudding dish (pan) and stick it
upside-down to the top of the TV. Glue
the ends of the knitting needles into the
top of the dish, to make an aerial.

6 Cut a rectangle of coloured paper
and glue it to the space left for the
control panel. Glue three bottle tops
to the panel to make control buttons.

Peg (Clothespin) Donkey

You will sometimes find an item that reminds you of something else, for example, an upside down old-fashioned clothes peg (clothespin) looks very like a donkey's head. The right way up, it makes a good leg, as the ends look like hooves. This little donkey is made from five wooden clothes pegs (clothespins) and a toilet-roll tube, and it looks very effective when painted.

YOU WILL NEED
toilet-roll tube
thin card (posterboard) scraps
pencil
scissors
strong, non-toxic glue
5 old-fashioned wooden
   clothes pegs (clothespins)
elastic bands
corrugated cardboard scraps
purple, white and brown
   poster paints
paintbrushes
paint-mixing container

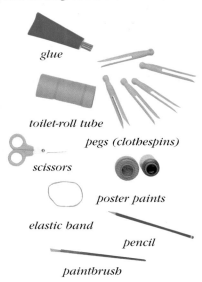

glue

toilet-roll tube

pegs (clothespins)

scissors

poster paints

elastic band

pencil

paintbrush

1 Stand the end of the toilet-roll tube on a scrap of thin card (posterboard). Draw round it twice. Cut out the circles and glue one to each end of the tube.

2 Glue four pegs (clothespins) to the toilet roll, two at each end. Hold in place with elastic bands while the glue dries.

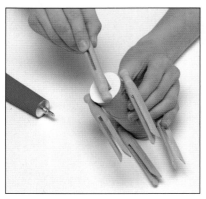

3 Cut a small strip of corrugated cardboard. Glue it to one end of the toilet roll. Glue a peg (clothespin) to the cardboard to make the head.

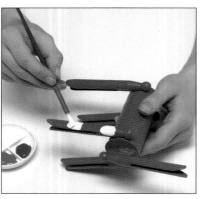

4 Paint the donkey purple. When the paint has dried, add white markings and the donkey's eyes. Paint its ears and hooves brown.

Pull-along Snake

This slithery snake is very simple to make from plastic bags, straws and a small yogurt pot. Plastic bags come in all sorts of bright colours; so, if you see a nice one, keep it.

YOU WILL NEED
scissors
green and yellow carrier bags
green and yellow drinking straws
thin coloured cord
3 wooden beads
small yogurt pot
pencil
thin cardboard (posterboard)
darning needle
PVA (white) glue
red plastic bag

wooden beads

plastic bags

glue

drinking straws

pencil

cord

yogurt pot

scissors

1 Cut sections from the green and yellow plastic bags. Cut circles of plastic from the bags. You will need about 15 of each colour. Fold each circle in four and snip the point to make a hole.

2 Cut 1-cm (½-in) pieces of yellow and green straws. You will need about 20 of each colour. Cut a long length of cord and tie a knot in the end. Thread a bead onto the cord and then six pieces of straw. Thread on a green circle and then a green straw, followed by a yellow circle and yellow straw. Keep on threading until you have used up all the pieces.

3 To make the head, cut the rim from a yogurt pot. Draw around the rim of the pot onto thin card (posterboard) and cut out the shape. Ask an adult to help you to make a hole in the centre of the card and the bottom of the pot.

4 Thread the card onto the cord and then the pot. Glue the card to the pot's rim. Tie a knot above the pot. Glue a forked tongue, cut from the red bag, to the bottom of the pot and two green beads to the top for the eyes.

Snake Sock Puppets

One good way to give your old socks a new lease of life is to make them into puppets. These snakes are decorated with brightly coloured felt. Once you've made a snake, why not make some other characters to keep it company?

YOU WILL NEED
coloured felt scraps
scissors
PVA (white) glue
1 sock

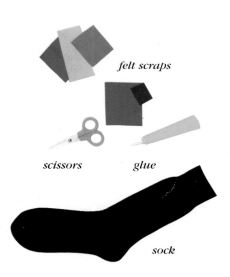

felt scraps

scissors　　*glue*

sock

1 To make the snake's eyes, cut two circles of felt. Cut two smaller circles of a different colour and glue them to the middle of the larger circles.

2 Glue the snake's eyes in position at the top of the sock.

3 Cut diamonds and strips of felt in various colours. Glue the strips at equal distances along the length of the sock. Glue the diamonds between the strips.

4 Cut a forked tongue from red felt. Glue the tongue to the top of the toe of the sock, in the centre. Allow the glue to dry thoroughly before you play with your sock puppet.

Wooden Spoon Puppets

You can make puppets from all sorts of things, but wooden spoons are especially good because they are just the right shape to make a head and a body. Gather a piece of fabric to hide the spoon handle, paint a face at the top and away you go!

YOU WILL NEED
wooden spoon
pink, blue, brown and yellow
  poster paints
paintbrush
paint-mixing container
pencil
ruler
fabric
scissors
darning needle
matching thread
strong, non-toxic glue
satin ribbon scrap
gold and coloured foil

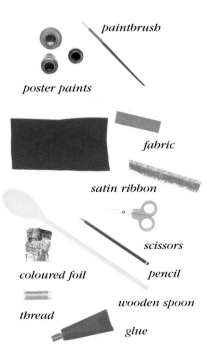

paintbrush

poster paints

fabric

satin ribbon

scissors

coloured foil

pencil

thread

wooden spoon

glue

1 Paint the top half of the wooden spoon pink and leave it to dry. Draw the puppet's eyes, nose, mouth and hair in pencil on the spoon and then fill in its features using poster paints.

2 Cut a piece of fabric as long as the spoon handle and 30 cm (12 in) wide. Sew a line of running stitches along the top edge of the fabric and pull the threads tight to gather the material. Knot the ends of the threads together.

3 Glue the gathered edge of the fabric around the spoon handle, below the puppet's face. Glue a short scrap of satin ribbon around the puppet's neck, to cover the top of the gathered fabric.

4 Cut a crown from gold foil and glue it to the top of the head. Cut two circles of coloured foil and glue one to the middle of the crown and one at the centre of the satin ribbon, as "jewels".

Pop-up Puppet

Make a pop-up puppet from an old wooden spoon and a plastic flowerpot. This puppet is a cat, but you can make all sorts of different characters using the same basic instructions.

YOU WILL NEED
ruler
orange felt
scissors
flowerpot
dressmaker's pins
darning needle
thread
strong, non-toxic glue
orange, red and blue poster paint
medium and fine paintbrushes
paint-mixing container
long-handled wooden spoon
felt-tipped pen
small bell
thin coloured cord
coloured sticky-paper dots

RECYCLING TIP
Ask permission before you raid the kitchen for wooden spoons.

orange felt
flowerpot
glue
scissors
cord
pins
sticky-paper dots
felt-tipped pen
thread
bell
paintbrushes
poster paints
wooden spoon

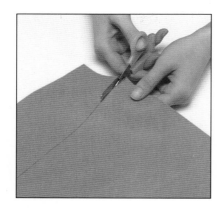

1 Cut a piece of felt measuring 20 cm (8 in) wide and long enough to fit around the inside of the flowerpot with 2 cm (¾ in) to spare.

2 Fold the felt in half widthways. Pin the two shorter sides of the fabric together. Sew the edges of the felt together, using small running stitches. Sew a line of long running stitches along the long edge of the felt. Leave the threads long to gather up the fabric.

3 Glue the folded long edge of the felt around the inside of the flowerpot, with the edge to be gathered at the top.

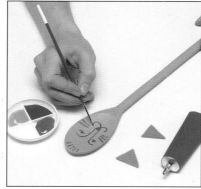

4 Paint a long-handled wooden spoon orange. When dry, draw the cat's features with the felt-tipped pen, then paint them with the fine paintbrush. Cut two triangles of orange felt and glue them to the top to make the cat's ears.

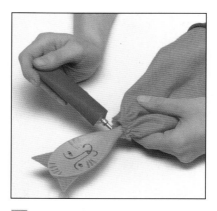

5 Pass the handle through the hole in the bottom of the pot. Pull the threads in the top of the felt tight to gather it together, and knot the ends. Put a little glue around the top of the handle and stick the gathered edge of the felt to it.

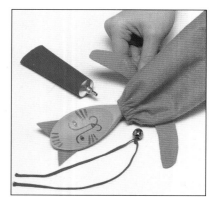

6 Cut two arms from scraps of felt and glue one to each side of the cat's body. Put a small bell on a length of coloured cord and tie it around the cat's neck. Decorate the rim of the flowerpot with a row of sticky dots.

Glove Puppets

If you've lost one of a pair of gloves and don't know what to do with the other, why not make this funny puppet family and their pet bird? Their hair is made from scraps of coloured cotton and their faces are little beads and other odds and ends. Scraps of felt are used to make the puppets really colourful.

You will need
thick blue and green thread
darning needle
1 glove
scissors
thin satin ribbon
fine felt-tipped pen
felt scraps
PVA (white) glue
small beads and buttons

glove

beads and buttons

scissors

thin satin ribbon

felt scraps

cotton thread

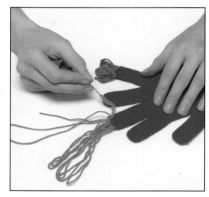

1 To make the blue hair on the little finger, sew loops of blue thread into the top edge of the finger. Make a small stitch after each loop to keep it in place.

2 To make the plaited hair, sew long loops of green thread into the top edge of the third finger. Make a small stitch after each loop to keep it in place.

3 Snip the ends of the green loops and trim the thread so that it is straight. Plait the thread and tie the ends with the satin ribbon.

4 Draw the hair, bow-tie and all the other shapes on scraps of felt, using the felt-tipped pen. Cut them out.

5 Glue the felt shapes to the front of the fingers, using PVA (white) glue.

6 Arrange all the beads and other bits and pieces on the puppets and glue them in place. Let the glue dry thoroughly before you play with your glove puppets.

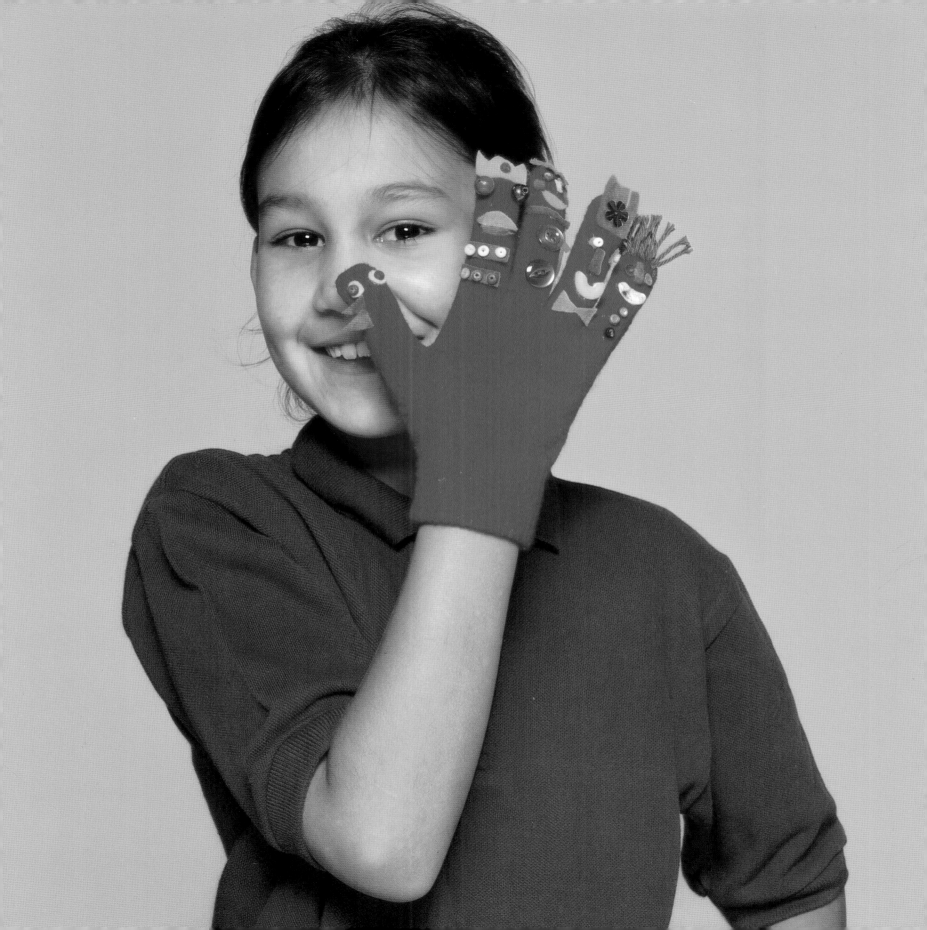

Pinball Table

Make this exciting pinball game and you'll have hours of fun! The bollards are made from small cotton reels (spools) and yogurt pots and the marble is kept on the table by elastic bands. Ask an adult to get you some strong, non-toxic glue, to stick the bollards to the table, otherwise the elastic bands will pull them off again.

TO PLAY PINBALL
The aim of the game is to keep the ball moving for as long as possible. Time how long it takes for it to reach the bottom of the table each time.

YOU WILL NEED
scissors
thin card (posterboard)
red, yellow and blue
  poster paints
paint-mixing container
paintbrush
PVA (white) glue
cotton reels (spools)
very strong, non-toxic glue
coloured sticky-paper dots
3 small yogurt cartons
foam board, measuring
  90 cm (36 in) x 60 cm (24 in)
pencil
thin coloured paper
long, thin, loose elastic bands
marble

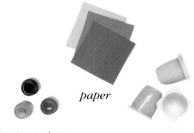

paper

poster paints   *yogurt pots*

marble

elastic bands

sticky-paper dots   *cotton reels (spools)*

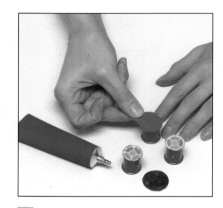

1 Cut a small circle of card to cover the top of each cotton reel (spool). Paint the card circles in bright colours.

2 Add a little PVA glue to some red poster paint. Paint all the reels (spools) red and leave them to dry. Glue a coloured circle to the top of each reel (spool) and stick a dot in the centre.

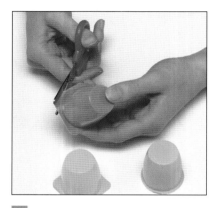

3 Carefully cut away the rims of the yogurt cartons leaving a narrow, trimmed edge. This will prevent the marble from catching on the rims.

4 Mark the positions for the bollards on the board. Put two under the top corners, so the board slopes. Glue them all in place and leave to dry overnight.

Draw numbers, arrows and stars on scraps of coloured paper. Cut them out and glue them to the table.

5 Draw numbers, arrows and stars on scraps of coloured paper. Cut them out and glue them to the table.

6 Stretch an elastic band between pairs of cotton reels (spools). Tie an elastic band between two bollards at the bottom to launch the marble.

Fruit Machine

Test your luck with this fun fruit machine. Each cotton reel (spool) has three symbols on it; spin them, and if they all show the same symbol award yourself a sweet.

YOU WILL NEED
cardboard cereal box
small cardboard box
pencil
scissors
paper glue
red, yellow and green thin paper
knitting needle with a
    rounded end
3 large cotton reels (spools)
4 small cotton reels (spools)
cork
pink and green poster paints
paintbrush
paint-mixing container
sweets

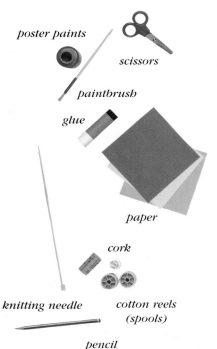

poster paints

scissors

paintbrush

glue

paper

cork

knitting needle

cotton reels (spools)

pencil

1 Open out the boxes and lay them flat. Draw three holes for the cotton reels (spools) on the front of the cereal box. Ask an adult to cut them out and make holes on the sides for the knitting needle. Draw a rectangle on the front of the smaller box and cut it out. Glue the boxes back together. Glue a rectangle of red paper to the back of the small box.

2 Cut three different-coloured strips of paper, as wide as the large cotton reels (spools) and long enough to fit around them. Cut out a triangle, a square and a circle in each of the three colours too.

3 Glue the yellow square, circle and triangle to the green strip, the red shapes to the yellow strip and the green shapes to the red. Glue a strip around each large reel (spool), to make the fruit machine's dials.

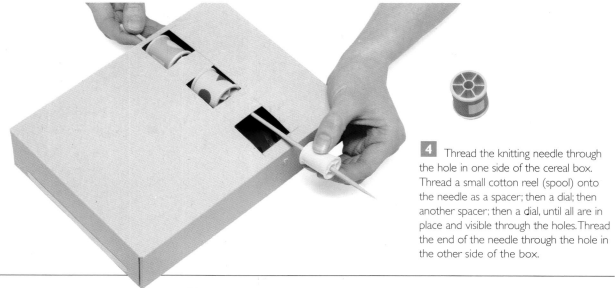

4 Thread the knitting needle through the hole in one side of the cereal box. Thread a small cotton reel (spool) onto the needle as a spacer; then a dial; then another spacer; then a dial, until all are in place and visible through the holes. Thread the end of the needle through the hole in the other side of the box.

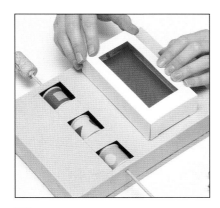

5 Glue the smaller box to the front of the fruit machine to make the prize box. Ask an adult to help you to push a cork onto the end of the knitting needle to keep it in place.

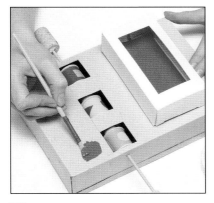

6 Paint the fruit machine pink and the prize box green. When the paint has dried, cut three small yellow stars and glue them to the top of the machine, above the holes. Fill the prize box with a selection of sweets.

Catch-the-ball Game

Test your skill with this bat-and-ball game. It takes quite a lot of practice to catch the ball in the cup but it's good fun while you are learning! Use a plastic bottle with a long neck, because this makes a better handle to hold on to.

YOU WILL NEED
coloured tissue paper
PVA (white) glue
mixing container
clear plastic bottle
scissors
yogurt pot
strong, non-toxic glue
thin coloured cord

tissue paper

paintbrush

yogurt pot   *strong glue*

cord

plastic bottle

1 Take two sheets of differently coloured tissue paper and tear them into strips and circles.

2 Mix some PVA (white) glue with a little water. Coat each strip of paper with glue. Cover the bottle with the paper. Add some circles of paper on top of the strips. Leave to dry thoroughly.

3 Carefully cut the corners from the top of the yogurt pot. Glue the pot to the centre of the bottle.

4 Roll a sheet of tissue paper tightly into a small ball. It should be small enough to fit inside the yogurt pot.

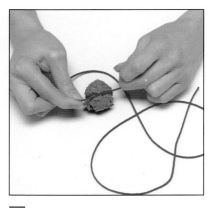

5 Cut a long piece of coloured cord. Tie one end of the cord tightly around the ball of tissue paper.

6 Tie the other end of the thin coloured cord around the end of the neck of the bottle.

Button Clacker

Button strings make a great clacking sound when you shake them against a cardboard tube. Collect old buttons and little beads as well, to make the strings look as interesting as possible. When you have finished, glue the plastic top back on to keep them in place.

YOU WILL NEED
orange, green and pink
    poster paints
paintbrushes
paint-mixing container
cardboard sweet (candy) tube,
    with a lid
darning needle
thin coloured cord
buttons and beads
strong, non-toxic glue

buttons and beads

needle

cord

glue

paintbrush

poster paints

sweet (candy) tube

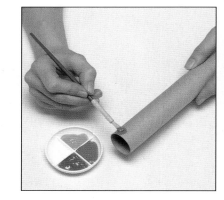

1 Paint the sweet (candy) tube with orange and green stripes. When the paint is dry, add pink spots.

2 Thread a darning needle with coloured cord. Tie a knot in the end of the cord and thread on a button. Sew in and out of the button a few more times. Thread on beads and buttons, until you have a string about 12 cm (5 in) long then make two more strings.

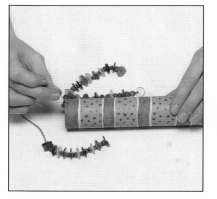

3 Ask an adult to make three holes in the top of the cardboard tube, leaving about 2.5 cm (1 in) between each hole. Then re-thread the needle with the end of one of the button strings.

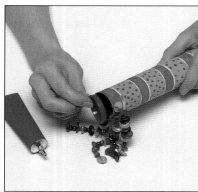

4 Push the needle through one of the holes in the top of the tube, then back through the holes in the button. Tie the end of the thread tightly around the button. Attach the other two strings, then glue the lid back on.

Rhythm Sticks

Thin pieces of branch make great percussion sticks. Look out for two sticks that are about the same length and thickness next time you are in a park or wood. Make sure the branches are really dry, so that they make a loud noise when you knock them together. If you wish, seal the surface of the sticks with non-toxic craft varnish after they have been painted.

YOU WILL NEED
2 sticks
white, red, green and yellow
  poster paints
paintbrush
paint-mixing container
scissors
coloured string

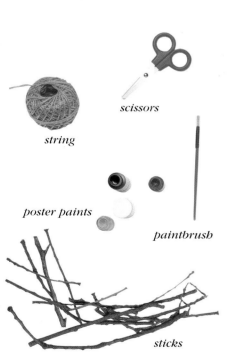

string

scissors

poster paints

paintbrush

sticks

1 Remove any leaves and loose bark from the sticks and paint them white. Leave the sticks to dry.

2 Paint decorative red and green spots on top of the white paint. Make the spots different sizes.

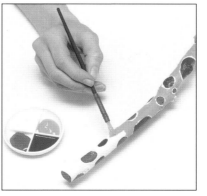

3 When the spots have dried, fill in the white space between them with yellow paint. Leave a small white space around each dot.

4 Cut two long pieces of coloured string. Tie one to the end of each stick. Wrap the string round and round the ends of the sticks to make handles. Tie the ends of the string very tightly so that they don't unravel.

Shaker

This shaker is filled with beads and buttons, but you can use rice or dried beans.

YOU WILL NEED
clear plastic bottle, with cap
small beads and buttons
large and small coloured
    sticky-paper dots
strong, non-toxic glue

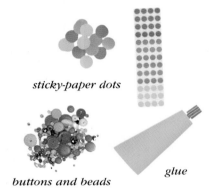

sticky-paper dots

buttons and beads   *glue*

1 Wash and carefully dry the bottle. It should be dry inside as well. Pour a mixture of small beads and buttons into the bottle. A couple of handfuls will make a good noise.

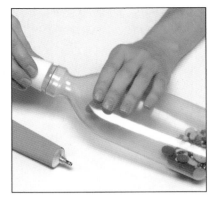

2 Spread a line of glue around the inside of the bottle top. Screw the top back onto the bottle. Stick coloured sticky-paper dots to the outside to make a bright and decorative pattern.

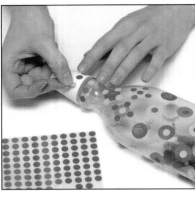

3 Stick a row of small coloured sticky-paper dots around the lower edge of the bottle top to make a pattern.

Tambourine

Two foil pie dishes can quickly and easily become a shiny tambourine.

YOU WILL NEED
ruler
thin satin ribbon
scissors
small bells
sticky tape
2 foil pie dishes (pans)
strong, non-toxic glue

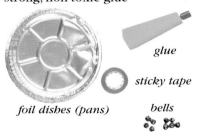

glue

sticky tape

foil dishes (pans)   *bells*

1 Cut 10-cm (3-in) lengths of ribbon and tie a bell to each piece.

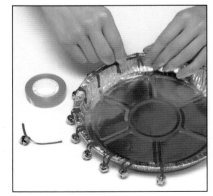

2 Tape the bells around the inside edge of one of the pie dishes (pans), making sure to space them evenly.

3 Spread glue around the rim of the second pie dish. Glue the two dishes together, rim to rim, covering the ends of the ribbons. Leave the glue to dry.

Drum

Drums are good fun to play and this one is portable, so you can play it wherever you are. The drum is made from an old plastic ice-cream tub and the drumsticks are knitting needles, with a wooden bead on the end.

YOU WILL NEED
ice-cream tub, with lid
yellow poster paint
paintbrush
paint-mixing container
PVA (white) glue
paper glue
scissors
coloured paper
thick coloured cord
dried rice
strong, non-toxic glue
2 large wooden beads
2 knitting needles

pencil

scissors

paper

glue

poster paint

ice-cream tub

wooden beads

cord

rice

1 Paint the outside of the ice-cream tub with bright poster paint mixed with a little PVA (white) glue. When the paint is dry, cut out squares of red paper and glue them around the tub.

2 Ask an adult to punch a hole in both sides of the tub. Cut a length of thick coloured cord and poke the ends through the holes in the tub. Tie a double knot in each end of the cord.

3 Put a handful of dried rice inside the tub and replace the lid. The rice will make a swishing sound when you beat the drum.

4 Cut a circle of red paper and glue it to the top of the lid of the drum.

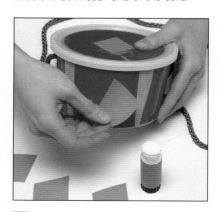

5 Cut diamonds of coloured paper. Glue one on top of each coloured square of paper around the sides of the drum and one to the top of the lid.

6 To make the drumsticks, use the strong glue to attach a large wooden bead to the end of each knitting needle. Let the glue dry thoroughly before you play your drum.

Groovy Guitar

Make yourself a groovy, twanging guitar from a cardboard tube and a washing-powder box. The strings are made from elastic bands and they rest on half a toilet-roll tube, which gives them quite loud different sounds.

YOU WILL NEED
washing-powder box
felt-tipped pen
scissors
long cardboard tube
brown-paper tape
toilet-roll tube
strong, non-toxic glue
yellow and orange poster paints
paintbrush
paint-mixing container
4 elastic bands
5 small cotton reels (spools)
silver foil
thick cord

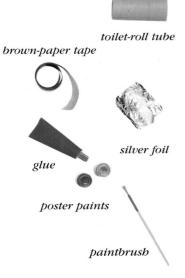

toilet-roll tube

brown-paper tape

silver foil

glue

poster paints

paintbrush

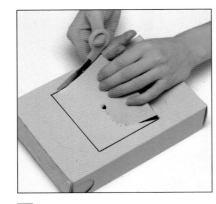

1 Draw a square on the front of the cardboard box. Ask an adult to help you to cut the square out of the box.

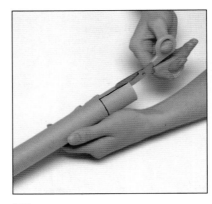

2 Draw a rectangle on one end of the cardboard tube. Ask an adult to help you cut the shape out of the tube, so that it will fit on the end of the box.

3 Put the tube on the end of the box and tape it in place with brown-paper tape to make the neck of the guitar.

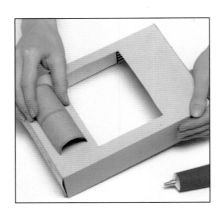

4 Cut a toilet-roll tube in half. Glue the half-tube below the hole in the front of the guitar.

5 When the paper tape and glue have dried, paint the guitar, using poster paints. Leave the guitar to dry thoroughly before playing.

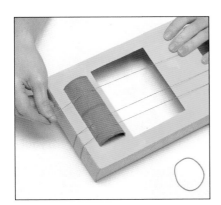

6 Stretch four elastic bands around the body of the guitar. Rest the elastic bands on the half toilet-roll, this will make them louder.

7 Cover five small cotton reels (spools) with silver foil, then glue four reels to the neck of the guitar to make pegs. Glue the other reel to the end of the guitar. Tie a length of cord from the neck of the guitar to the reel at the base of the guitar to make a strap.

Nail Chimes

Make beautiful music with these nifty nail chimes. They are suspended from a cardboard tube and, because they hang freely, they make a lovely, clear, ringing sound when you strike them. You will need to find bolts in various sizes, so that your chimes make different notes.

YOU WILL NEED
scissors
coloured paper
cardboard tube
paper glue
coloured sticky-paper dots
strong coloured cord
bolts of various sizes
1 long bolt

paper

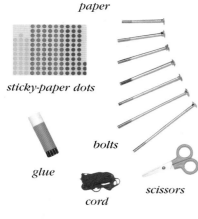

sticky-paper dots

glue

bolts

cord

scissors

cardboard tube

1 Cut a rectangle of coloured paper as long as the cardboard tube and wide enough to fit around it. Stick the paper to the tube.

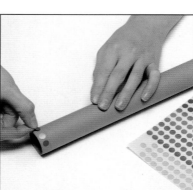

2 Stick a row of sticky-paper dots around each end of the cardboard tube, as decoration.

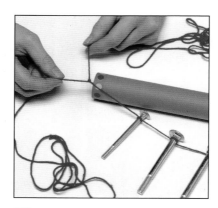

3 Cut a long length of coloured cord. It must be strong enough to bear the weight of all the bolts.

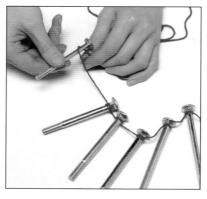

4 Tie the length of cord around the head of each bolt. Make sure that the bolts are evenly spaced along the cord.

5 Thread the free ends of the coloured cord through the cardboard tube. Tie them together at one end.

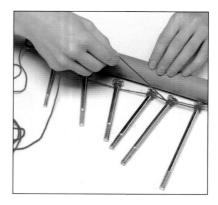

6 Loop one of the cords two or three times around the head of each bolt again, then pass it back through the tube. Tie the ends tightly together. Play the chimes using the long bolt.

Squeezy Bottle Dog Book-ends

These book-ends are made by covering two squeezy bottles with small pieces of papier-mâché and then painting. The legs are made from corks and the ears and tails are cut from scraps of thin card (posterboard).

YOU WILL NEED
2 squeezy bottles
funnel
dried rice
masking tape
newspaper
PVA (white) glue, diluted
8 corks
white, red, yellow, brown and
    black poster paints
paintbrushes
paint-mixing container
pencil
thin white card (posterboard)
scissors

squeezy bottle

masking tape

rice   *corks*   *scissors*

funnel

glue

poster paints

paintbrushes

1 Wash and dry the squeezy bottles. Put a funnel in the top of each bottle and half-fill it with rice. Seal the top of each bottle with a strip of masking tape.

2 Tear the newspaper into strips. Dip each strip in the PVA (white) glue and cover the bottles completely with two layers of paper. Leave the bottles to dry.

3 With PVA (white) glue, stick four corks to one side of each squeezy bottle to make the legs. Leave the book-ends to dry thoroughly.

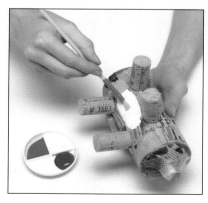

4 Paint the book-ends white. You may have to use two coats of paint to cover up the newsprint completely.

5 Draw in the faces, collars and markings with the pencil. Decorate the dogs using poster paints.

6 Draw four ears and two tails on the card (posterboard) and cut out. Bend back the edges of each shape and glue ears and a tail onto each dog, using the strong glue.

Nature Frame

This woody frame is made out of corrugated cardboard and covered with twigs and scraps of tree bark collected on a country walk. The frame has a "spacer" in the middle, so you can push pictures into the frame from the top. You could glue fir cones on top of the twigs to make the frame even more decorative.

RECYCLING TIP
You could stick other natural items round the frame, such as feathers and little pebbles.

YOU WILL NEED
ruler
pencil
corrugated cardboard
scissors
strong, non-toxic glue
short twigs and pieces of bark

corrugated cardboard

scissors   *glue*

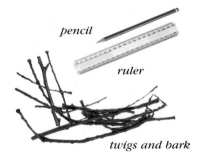

pencil
ruler

twigs and bark

1 Measure out the frame pieces on corrugated cardboard, following the pattern at the front of the book. Cut out the pieces.

2 Glue the spacer to the frame back. Make sure that the edges of the cardboard line up neatly.

3 Glue the front sections to the spacer to complete the frame.

4 Glue the twigs and pieces of bark around the frame. Choose each piece of wood carefully, so that it naturally follows the shape of the frame. Add more than one layer of twigs for greater effect.

5 Cut out a stand for the frame on a piece of cardboard.

6 Make a fold in the long side of the stand. Spread a little glue along the fold and stick the stand to the centre of the back of the frame. Allow to dry before you use your frame.

Cardboard Frame

Corrugated cardboard is great for making frames, because it is strong and smooth and you can paint it easily. You can make your frame any size you want, so look for the large cardboard boxes used for electrical equipment.

RECYCLING TIP
If you have a collection of pretty little shells you could use these to decorate the frame.

YOU WILL NEED
ruler
pencil
thick corrugated cardboard
scissors
thin corrugated cardboard
strong, non-toxic glue
red, green, yellow and blue
    poster paints
paintbrush
paint-mixing container

poster paints   *scissors*

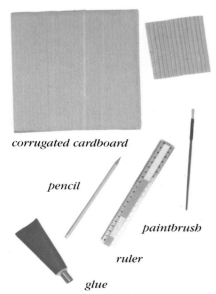

corrugated cardboard

pencil

ruler   *paintbrush*

glue

1 Measure and draw out the back of the frame and a spacer on a sheet of thick corrugated cardboard, following the pattern at the front of the book, then cut out.

2 Using the pattern at the front of the book, draw out the pieces that make the front of the frame on thin cardboard. Cut them out. Glue the spacer to the frame back. Glue front pieces to the spacer.

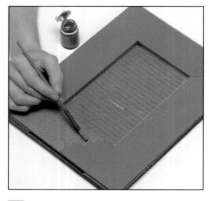

3 Paint the frame using poster paints. You may have to paint it twice to cover the cardboard completely.

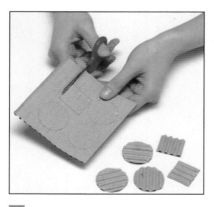

4 Cut circles and squares from the grooved side of a piece of thin corrugated cardboard.

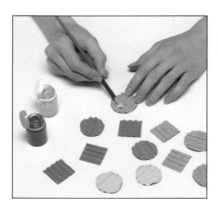

5 Paint the shapes in bright colours.

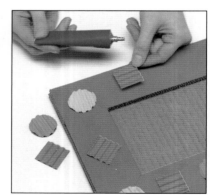

6 When the paint is completely dry, glue the circles and squares around the frame to make a decorative border.

Papier-mâché Bowl

Papier-mâché is like magic because you can make all sorts of things from it, using only old newspapers and glue. This bowl is decorated by gluing bright strips of wrapping paper and paper shapes to its surface, and is good for holding fruit or odds and ends.

YOU WILL NEED
petroleum jelly
plastic bowl
newspaper
PVA (white) glue, diluted
scissors
gift wrap
thin coloured paper
PVA (white) glue

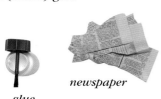

glue

newspaper

plastic bowl

coloured paper

scissors

1 Grease your chosen bowl with a thin coating of petroleum jelly, so that the papier-mâché bowl will come out. Tear newspaper into 2.5-cm (1-in) wide strips. Dip the strips in the diluted PVA (white) glue and press into the mould, overlapping the edges slightly. Press in six layers and leave to dry overnight.

2 Gently pull the paper shape out of the mould. Leave the bowl upside-down to dry. When it has dried, cut away the rough edges from the rim of the bowl.

3 Tear the gift wrap into strips and glue them to the outside and inside of the bowl to decorate it.

4 Cut circles from the coloured paper. Snip segments out of the paper to make "stars".

5 Glue the stars to the centre and sides of the bowl.

6 Cut lots of small squares from two colours of thin paper. Glue the squares around the outside edge of the bowl.

Appliquéd Scarf

Wool blankets are lovely and warm, so if you find an old one that no one wants anymore, why not make it into a cosy scarf?

YOU WILL NEED
measuring tape
piece of thin woollen blanket
scissors
orange, blue, green and pink felt
tracing paper
pencil
thin card (posterboard)
felt-tipped pen
dressmaker's pins
darning needle
bright, thick cotton thread

woollen blanket

felt

thick cotton thread

felt-tipped pen

scissors

1 Cut a piece of blanket measuring about 60 cm (24 in) × 90 cm (36 in). Fold it in half lengthways to make a long, narrow rectangle, so that the two long edges meet in the middle and overlap by 1.5 cm (½ in) on either side. Ask an adult to iron it, so the folds stay in place.

2 Cut six squares, 7 cm (2½ in) × 7 cm (2½ in), from orange and blue felt. Then cut six circles to fit inside the squares from green and pink felt. Cut six smaller circles from blue and green felt.

3 Draw a flower pattern on a piece of thin card (posterboard) and cut it out to make a template. Make six flowers by drawing around the template on scraps of felt. Cut them out.

4 Pin three squares to each end of the scarf and sew each square in place, using thick, bright cotton. Sew a large circle on top of each square. Place a flower and small circle in the centre of each circle, and sew them in place with a few small stitches.

5 Fold the scarf so the flowers are on the inside. Pin the long edges together and sew them, using small running stitches. Place the scarf flat with the seam down the middle. Pin the top and bottom edges together. Sew along the top edge and halfway along the bottom.

6 Turn the scarf the right way out. Turn the rest of the lower edges to the inside of the scarf. Carefully sew the edges together, using small stitches. Ask an adult to iron the seams flat for you.

Pompom Hat

Beat the cold with this fun pompom hat. It's made by cutting down an old pair of wool tights. Leftover balls of wool are used to make two pompoms to decorate the top of the hat and it looks so stylish that no one will be able to guess what it is made from.

YOU WILL NEED
measuring tape
pair of wool tights
scissors
darning needle
thin wool
pencil
pair of compasses
thin cardboard
knitting-wool oddments

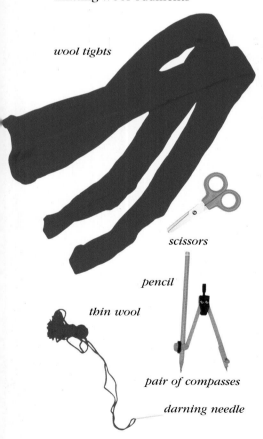

wool tights

scissors

pencil

thin wool

pair of compasses

darning needle

1 Measure 15 cm (6 in) down from the top of each leg of the tights. Cut off the legs at this point and discard them.

2 Thread the needle with the wool. Sew across the top of the cut ends, using small running stitches. Pull the stitching tight. Sew two more stitches to keep the ends gathered. Cut the thread.

3 Draw two identical circles with the pencil and pair of compasses on the cardboard. Draw smaller circles inside. Cut out the larger circles. Ask an adult to help you to cut out the smaller ones.

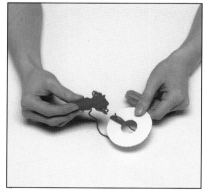

4 Place the circles together. Tie the end of a length of wool around the circles. Wrap the wool around and around the circles, passing it through the central hole, until the hole is filled in.

5 Snip through the wool at the edge of the circles. Pull the circles slightly apart and tie a short piece of wool around the centre of the wool between the circles, to keep it all together. Pull the circles off and trim any uneven wool.

6 Make a second pompom, then sew one to the end of each gathered leg. Roll up the waistband a couple of times to make a brim, and tie the legs loosely together to wear the hat.

Storage Chest

This small storage chest is great for keeping little treasures safe. It is made from large, empty matchboxes and is covered with scraps of sticky-backed plastic. You can make the chest as large as you want – just keep adding more matchboxes. You can also use large and small matchboxes, so you have different-size compartments.

RECYCLING TIP
This is an ideal storage place for those buttons, beads, pins and paper clips that all good recyclers collect and keep.

YOU WILL NEED
green and red sticky-backed
  plastic
scissors
6 large matchboxes
strong, non-toxic glue
tracing paper
pencil
thin card (posterboard)
6 coloured plastic beads

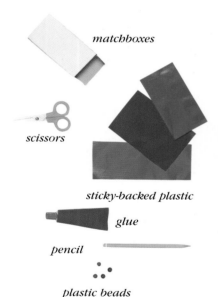

matchboxes

scissors

sticky-backed plastic

glue

pencil

plastic beads

1 Cut three green and three red pieces of sticky-backed plastic the same width and long enough to fit around a matchbox, and stick them on.

2 Cut six thin strips of red and six of green sticky-backed plastic. Stick them to the front and back of the box trays; red in green boxes and green in red boxes.

3 Spread glue along the long side of one green box and glue it to a red box, and repeat so that you have three rows of two boxes.

4 When the glue has dried, glue the three rows of boxes on top of each other to make the storage chest. Make sure that the edges of the boxes line up.

5 Trace the pattern for the decoration; lay it face-down on a piece of card (posterboard); draw over the lines to transfer and cut it out. Cover the card with sticky-backed plastic and trim.

6 Cut out a small red heart and stick it to the front of the decoration. Bend back the decoration's base and glue it to the top of the chest. Glue a plastic bead to the front of each tray for handles.

Printed Stationery

Personal stationery is often very expensive, but you can make your own by printing it with these simple printing blocks. The pad of each block is made from shapes cut from washing-up sponges. Once you are used to the technique, make some blocks with your initials on.

YOU WILL NEED
pencil
ruler
thick corrugated cardboard
scissors
strong, non-toxic glue
felt-tipped pen
washing-up sponge
poster paints
paintbrush (optional)
saucer
coloured writing paper

washing-up sponge

writing paper

corrugated cardboard

pencil

glue

ruler

poster paints

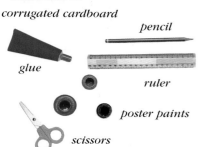

scissors

1 Draw three 5 cm (2 in) by 5 cm (2 in) squares and three 4 cm (1½ in) by 4 cm (1½ in) squares on the corrugated cardboard. Cut out all the squares.

2 Glue the small squares upright on top of the larger squares to make printing blocks (the small squares are the handles for holding the blocks).

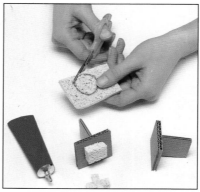

3 With a felt-tipped pen, draw simple shapes onto the washing-up sponge. Cut out the shapes and glue one to each printing block.

4 When the glue has dried, spread a little thick paint on a saucer. Dip a block into the paint or use the brush to coat it, so that the sponge is coated, and then press the block firmly onto a piece of writing paper to print the shape.

Patchwork Pencil Case

This bright pencil case is made in a patchwork design. Patchwork is a great way to use up small scraps of pretty fabric.

YOU WILL NEED
pencil
ruler
thin card (posterboard) scraps
scissors
felt scraps
felt-tipped pen
darning needle
brightly coloured thread
dressmaker's pins
press studs
8 buttons

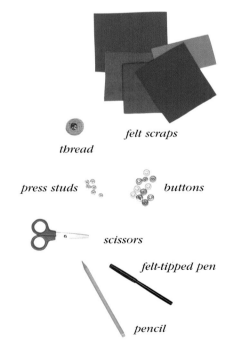

felt scraps

thread

press studs   *buttons*

scissors

felt-tipped pen

pencil

1 Draw a square measuring 6 cm (2½ in) by 6 cm (2½ in) on thin card (posterboard). Cut out the square to make a template. Draw round the template onto 16 scraps of coloured felt.

2 Place the edges of two felt squares together. Sew the squares together with brightly coloured thread, using small running stitches. Sew on two more squares to make a row of four squares. Make another three separate rows of four felt squares. Place the four rows together and join each row with small running stitches to make a large patchwork square.

4 Fold the top and bottom edges of the patchwork over. Sew along the folded edges, using small running stitches. Fold the patchwork square in half lengthways. Pin and sew the sides together. Sew press studs along the opening in the top of the pencil case.

5 Cut small squares from the leftover felt and sew a button to the centre of each one, then sew one to the centre of each square on the front of the case.

JEWELLERY AND DECORATIONS

Jam Jar Lid Badges

Next time you finish a jar of jam, keep the lid to make a fun badge. Cover the lids in silver foil and then cut shapes from scraps of bright foil, saved from sweet wrappers. You can buy special badge pins but a safety pin is fine.

YOU WILL NEED
scissors
silver foil
strong, non-toxic glue
jam jar lid
coloured foil scraps
safety pin
sticky tape

safety pin

sticky tape

foil scraps

jam-jar lid *silver foil*

glue

scissors

1 Cut a square of foil that is about 4 cm (1½ in) larger all the way round than the jam jar lid. Spread glue on the back of the lid and then wrap it in the foil. Squash the foil down on the inside of the lid.

2 Cut a circle of gold foil and glue it to the inside of the lid. Cut shapes from scraps of coloured foil and glue them on top of the gold circle.

3 As a change, snip the edges of the gold foil circle to make a "star".

4 Turn the badge over and put a safety pin in the centre. Tape the pin in place to make a fastener.

Squeezy Bottle Bracelets

Sections of a squeezy bottle are perfect for making bracelets and bangles, and you can decorate them in lots of different ways. Scraps of coloured foil saved from sweet wrappers make really bright, cheerful stripes and you can also roll the foil to make glittery fake jewels.

YOU WILL NEED
squeezy bottle
scissors
sticky tape
silver foil
coloured foil scraps
strong, non-toxic glue

silver foil

foil scraps

scissors

glue

squeezy bottle

1 Wash and dry an empty squeezy bottle. Ask an adult to help you to cut a 2.5 cm (1 in) wide section from the bottle that is long enough to go round your wrist comfortably. Join the ends of the section together, using sticky tape, to make a bangle.

2 Cut a piece of silver foil about twice the width of the bangle. Place the bangle on the foil and press the foil around the bangle to cover it.

3 Smooth the scraps of coloured foil with your fingers. Cut several strips of foil long enough to fit around the bangle. Glue the strips around the bangle at equal distances.

4 Roll more scraps of different coloured foil into small beads and glue them around the outside of the bangle to make "jewels".

Rolled-paper Beads

Gift wrap comes in lovely designs and can be used in lots of different ways once you have finished unwrapping your presents! Brightly coloured paper makes wonderful beads, if you roll it around a pencil. Ask your family and friends to save all their scraps for you, and make an exciting and colourful necklace.

YOU WILL NEED
ruler
pencil
gift wrap
scissors
paper glue
thin elastic

gift wrap

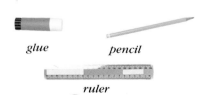

glue   *pencil*

ruler

scissors

1 Draw lots of 2.5 cm (1 in) wide strips on the back of a sheet of gift wrap. Make a mark halfway along one short edge of each strip. Draw lines from the two opposite corners to the marked point, dividing the strip into three long, thin triangles.

2 Cut along the lines on each strip.

3 Starting at the bottom of the triangle, roll the strips of paper around a pencil. Roll them carefully, so the bead is even and the edges are neat.

4 Put a little glue on the end of the paper. Wrap the end over the bead and press it down. Leave the bead on the pencil until the glue is dry. When you have enough beads, thread them onto a length of elastic and knot the ends.

Foil-bead Pendant

Silver foil makes great jewellery. You can roll it into little balls to make sparkling "jewels", or make long, thin beads like these, which are rolled around a pencil. A paper clip taped to the back of the pendant makes a handy hanger to suspend the beads from.

YOU WILL NEED
ruler
pencil
silver foil
scissors
thin card (posterboard)
strong, non-toxic glue
coloured foil
sequins
gold sticky-paper star
sticky tape
paper clip
thin coloured cord

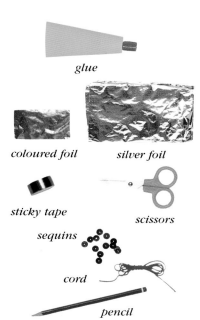

glue

coloured foil   silver foil

sticky tape

scissors

sequins

cord

pencil

1 Cut rectangles of foil measuring 30 cm (12 in) long and 2.5 cm (1 in) wide. Roll each strip around a pencil to make a bead. Glue the edges together. You will need 20 beads altogether.

2 Draw a circle on a piece of thin card (posterboard). Cut out the circle and glue coloured foil to each side of it to make the pendant.

3 Glue different-coloured sequins around the edge of the pendant. Add a gold sticky-paper star to the centre of the circle. Tape a paper clip to the back of the pendant to make a hanger.

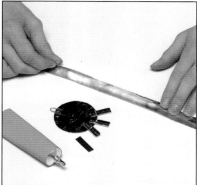

4 Cut a foil strip 20 cm (8 in) × 2.5 cm (1 in); fold in half lengthways and in half again; glue the edges. Cut it into 2.5-cm (1-in) lengths. Glue them to the lower edge of the pendant's back. Thread the beads and pendant onto the cord.

Sponge-flower Hairband

Washing-up sponges come in such pretty colours that it seems a pity not to use them in new ways. Here, pink, yellow and green sponges have been used to make a flower to decorate and brighten up a plain hairband.

YOU WILL NEED
tracing paper
pencil
thin card (posterboard)
scissors
yellow, pink and green
    washing-up sponges
thin black felt-tipped pen
darning needle
yellow, pink and green or
    blue threads
hairband

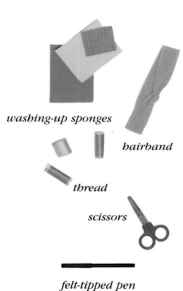

washing-up sponges

hairband

thread

scissors

felt-tipped pen

1 Trace the flower patterns from the front of the book. Lay the tracings, face-down, on the card (posterboard) and draw over the lines again. Cut out the shapes to make a template.

2 Place the flower template on the yellow sponge, the flower centre on the pink sponge and the leaves on the green sponge. Draw around the templates using the felt-tipped pen and then cut out the shapes.

3 Place the pink flower centre in the middle of the flower. Sew the centre to the flower with three or four small stitches, using pink thread.

4 Place the leaves, pointing outwards, on the front of the hairband. Sew the stems to the band with small stitches of blue or green thread. Lay the flower on top of the stems, and sew its centre and edges to the band with yellow thread.

Nature Box

If you go for an autumn walk in the countryside or a park you will probably find twigs, seed pods, fir cones and so on, which make lovely decorations. This plain cardboard box has been painted green and then rows of acorns, seed pods and small and large fir cones have been added to make it really decorative. Always ask an adult to look at what you have found to see that it is safe. Carefully wash everything before you use it.

YOU WILL NEED
green poster paint
paintbrush
paint-mixing container
cardboard box, with lid
acorns, fir cones and seed pods
strong, non-toxic glue

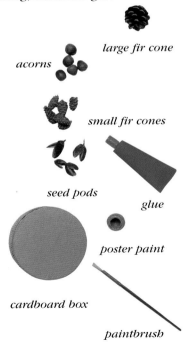

large fir cone

acorns

small fir cones

seed pods

glue

poster paint

cardboard box

paintbrush

1 Paint the lid and base of the cardboard box with poster paint and leave it to dry thoroughly.

2 Arrange a row of acorns around the edge of the lid of the box and glue them in position.

3 Glue a large fir cone to the middle of the lid. Glue small fir cones to the top of the lid, between the acorns and the large fir cone.

4 Glue a row of seed pods at equal distances around the sides of the box. Let the glue dry thoroughly before you use your box.

Fabric Scrap Picture

Raid the sewing basket to find scraps of colourful fabric to make a picture. You will need a fairly large piece of material to make the background and smaller pieces to make the hen and the trees. If you don't have any special fabric glue, use PVA (white) glue instead.

YOU WILL NEED
ruler
coloured cardboard
scissors
fabric scraps
tracing paper
pencil
thin card (posterboard)
thin black felt-tipped pen
fabric or PVA (white) glue

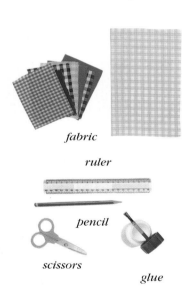

fabric

ruler

pencil

scissors

glue

1 Cut a rectangle of coloured cardboard measuring 25 cm (10 in) × 30 cm (12 in). Cut a piece of fabric 23 cm (9 in) × 28 cm (11 in). Glue together.

2 Make templates by tracing the patterns from the front of the book on to thin card (posterboard) with a felt-tipped pen. Cut them out.

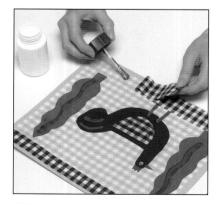

3 Draw around the tree template on two scraps of green fabric, using a thin black felt-tipped pen. Cut out the trees and glue one to each end of the picture.

4 Put the chicken template on blue fabric and the wing on blue checked fabric. Draw around them, using the felt-tipped pen and cut them out. Glue the chicken's body to the centre of the picture. Glue its wing on top of its body.

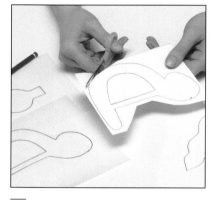

5 Cut the chicken's legs, face and feet from scraps of fabric and glue them in place. Cut long, wavy strips of red fabric to make the patterns on the trees, and glue them in place.

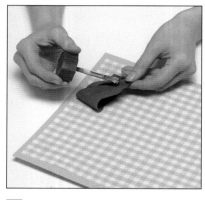

6 Glue a strip of green checked fabric to the bottom of the picture for grass, and a strip of blue checked fabric to the top for the sky. Cut a circle of red checked fabric for the sun and use small scraps of red fabric for its rays.

Straw Mobile

Drinking straws come in wonderful bright colours and you can use them to make lots of different projects. This mobile is made from pieces of straw threaded together.

YOU WILL NEED
scissors
coloured drinking straws
ruler
coloured cotton cord
strong, non-toxic glue
large buttons
wooden beads

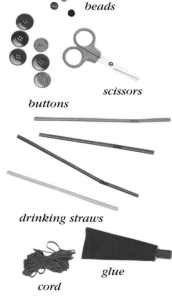

beads

scissors

buttons

drinking straws

glue

cord

1 Cut four different-coloured straws into 12-cm (4-in) pieces. Cut a long piece of coloured cord and thread the straw pieces onto it. Tie the ends of the cord, so that the straws make a square.

2 Cut more straws into 2.5-cm (1-in) lengths. Tie a length of coloured cord at each corner of the straw square. Thread the pieces of straw onto the cotton.

3 Tie the pieces of cotton together at the top. Tie another length of cord to the top of the mobile and thread some more short lengths of straw onto it.

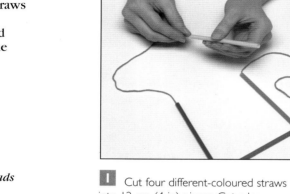

4 Cut four 2.5-cm (1-in) pieces and one 5-cm (2-in) piece of the same coloured straw. Glue the longer piece of straw to the back of a large button. Glue two short pieces of straw on each side of the long piece. Glue another button on top to make a star. Make four more stars in different colours.

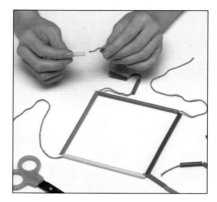

5 Cut four different lengths of coloured cord and tie one to each corner of the square, so that they hang down. Cut 2.5-cm (1-in) lengths of straw and thread them onto the cotton. Thread a star onto the end of each cord and one on the top of the mobile.

6 Thread a wooden bead on the end of each piece of cord, to keep the stars in place. Knot the ends of the four cords that hang down and trim the ends. Leave a long cord at the top of the mobile to make a hanger.

Pine Cone Mobile

Pine cones are lovely objects and they look great suspended from a mobile. The bars of this mobile are made from lengths of twig and the pine cones are tied at different heights. Pine cones are very much a part of winter, and you could paint your twigs and cones with gold or silver poster paint to make a Christmas mobile.

YOU WILL NEED
scissors
thin coloured cord
pine cones
2 thin twigs and 1 forked twig

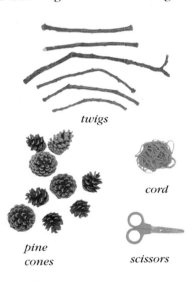

twigs

pine cones

cord

scissors

1 Cut lengths of cord and attach each one to the top of a cone. Tie a cone to both ends of two short twigs.

2 Tie the two twigs together with the cord, one above the other, to make the mobile shape.

3 Tie more small pine cones to the llower section of the mobile. Hang them at different heights.

4 Tie a large forked twig to the upper twig. Wrap the two together tightly by winding cord around them. Tie a length of cord to the top of the mobile to make a hanger.

Felt-scrap Christmas Cards

There are always lots of leftover scraps when you make something out of felt. Its a pity to waste them, even if they're quite small, because you can use them to make bright greetings cards. Save scraps of coloured paper and card, as well, to make backings for the cards.

YOU WILL NEED
pencil
ruler
thin coloured card (posterboard)
scissors
fine felt-tipped pen
scraps of coloured felt
PVA (white) glue

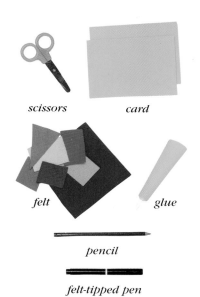

scissors   *card*

felt   *glue*

pencil

felt-tipped pen

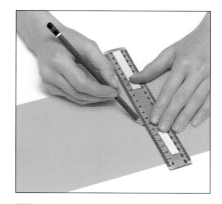

1 Draw a rectangle measuring 22 cm (9 in) × 15 cm (6 in) on the card. Cut out the rectangle and fold it in half.

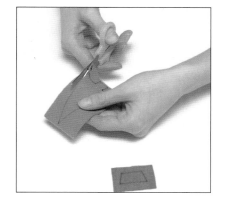

2 Draw a tree shape on a scrap of green felt and a tub on a piece of pink felt, using the fine felt-tipped pen. Cut out the shapes.

3 Cut a rectangle of blue felt slightly smaller than the card backing. Glue the tree and the tub to the blue felt.

4 Glue the picture to the front of the card. Cut small circles of coloured felt to make baubles and glue them to the tree.

Paper-clip Christmas Decorations

These shiny Christmas decorations will add a sparkle to your Christmas tree. Decorate them with scraps of bright foil from sweet wrappers, and sandwich paper clips between them to make the decorations look like icicles.

YOU WILL NEED
pencil
pair of compasses
thin card (posterboard)
scissors
silver foil
coloured foil
strong, non-toxic glue
silver paper clips
thin silver elastic

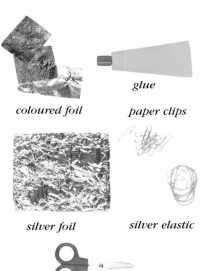

coloured foil   *glue*

paper clips

silver foil   *silver elastic*

scissors

1 Using a pencil and a pair of compasses, draw two circles exactly the same size on the card (posterboard), and then cut them out.

2 Cut two squares of silver foil about 4 cm (1½ in) bigger all the way around than the circles of card. Place a circle in the middle of each piece of foil. Wrap the edges of the silver foil over the card (posterboard).

3 Cut a circle of coloured foil and snip small triangles from its edges to make a "star" shape. Glue the star to the front of one of the card circles. Cut two circles from coloured foil and glue them to the middle of the star.

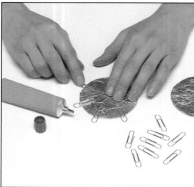

4 Glue a row of paper clips to the back of the other circle. Glue the two circles together. Tie a length of thin silver elastic to the top of the decoration to make a hanger.

Pasta-shape Christmas Tree Decorations

These Christmas-tree decorations are made from plastic pudding cartons. They are painted in bright colours and then decorated with pieces of dried pasta, which comes in lots of lovely shapes and sizes. Mix the paint with PVA (white) glue first, so that it sticks to the plastic.

YOU WILL NEED
2 plastic pudding cartons
PVA (white) glue
green, gold and pink
    poster paints
paintbrush
dried pasta shapes
2 gold pipe cleaners
strong, non-toxic glue

glue

poster paint

paintbrush

gold pipe cleaners

dried pasta shapes

1 Wash and dry the cartons. Mix a little glue with green poster paint and paint one carton. Repeat with pink paint and the second carton. When dry, paint the top and bottom edges gold.

2 Paint the pasta shapes you have chosen with gold poster paint. Leave them to dry thoroughly.

3 Ask an adult to help you to make a hole in the top of the cartons. Push both ends of the pipe cleaners through the holes. On the inside of the dishes, bend the ends of the pipe cleaners outwards to keep them in place.

4 Spread a little glue around the edge of each pasta shape. Glue the shapes around the sides of the cartons. Thread a pasta shape over the top of each pipe cleaner and glue them to the top of the decoration.

Christmas Door Hanging

This cheerful door-decoration is easy to make from foil pie dishes (pans) and clothes pegs (clothespins). Silver foil always looks Christmassy and the smiling snowman will brighten up any door or window.

VARIATION

Any picture could go in the middle – try a gold star or a jolly Father Christmas.

YOU WILL NEED
pencil
thin coloured and white paper
scissors
paper glue
7 small foil pie dishes (pans)
strong, non-toxic glue
7 plastic clothes pegs
   (clothespins)
large foil pie dish (pan)
coloured ribbon

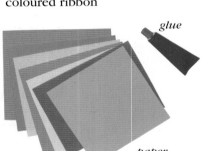
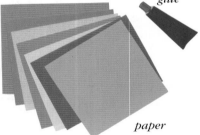

glue

paper

pencil

foil dishes (pans)

ribbon

scissors

*clothes pegs
(clothespins)*

1 Draw circles the same size as the bottoms of the small pie dishes (pans) on the paper and cut them out.

2 With paper glue, glue the paper circles to the centres of the small pie dishes. Cut stars from scraps of the paper and glue one to the centre of each circle.

3 Using the strong glue, stick each of the small pie dishes to the top of a plastic clothes peg (clothespin).

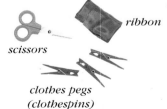

4 Draw and cut out a large circle of coloured paper to cover the bottom of the large dish. Glue it in place.

5 Cut a snowman from white paper and glue him to the middle of the large pie dish. Cut his hat, face, arms and buttons from scraps of coloured paper and glue them in place.

6 Clip the small pie dishes around the larger one, using the pegs. Tape a piece of coloured ribbon to the back of the large pie dish to make a hanger.

INDEX

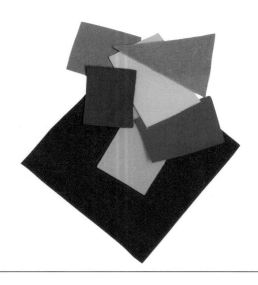